Jesus Loves You

Story by Noah Jacobson
Illustrated by Bonnie J. Jacobson

Jesus Loves You

ISBN: 978-0-578-39015-4

Copyright © 2022 by Noah Jacobson and Bonnie J. Jacobson

All rights reserved. Lion of Judah Publishing, Minnesota, USA

Story by Noah Jacobson

Illustrated by Bonnie J. Jacobson

Publishing services provided by BelieversBookServices.com

Printed in the United States of America

First Edition 2022

For more information about this book or its authors, please contact Lion of Judah Publishing:

Noah Jacobson
noahjacobson21@icloud.com

Bonnie J. Jacobson
bonniejoy55802@gmail.com

Dedicated to ___HAZEL___

From ___GRANDMA SHELLY + GRANDPA TAD___

Date ___8/27/22___

In the Beginning...

God created the Heavens and the Earth.
He made the sun and the moon, too.
He keeps us warm and gives us light.
When you see the sun in the sky,
remember, He loves you!

(Genesis 1:1-19)

God told Noah to build a boat.
Noah listened to God, and one day, just
like God promised, it started to rain.
He loaded all of the animals two by two.

Noah's Ark

There was a big flood, but because Noah listened, all of the animals were saved. Listen to God, because He will always be there for you.

(Genesis 6-8:19)

7

Look! A Rainbow!

At the end of the flood, a rainbow appeared. God promised He would never create a giant flood again. He always keeps His promises and sends a rainbow after every storm to remind us.
When you see a rainbow, remember that He will always keep His promises.

(Genesis 9:12-17)

The waves crashed against the boat. The waves were too strong, and the disciples thought they were going to sink. They started to get scared! They ran down into the boat and woke up Jesus.

The Storm

Jesus told them not to worry,
and He made the sea calm.
When you see waves, remember the
power of Jesus to calm the sea.

(Mark 4:35-41)

Flowers

Flowers are beautiful and blossom
into many shapes and sizes.
Some are tall,
some are short,
but they are all made perfectly.
You are like a flower.
No matter what you look like,
you are beautiful.
Whenever you see flowers,
remember God made you that
way, because that is His
superpower.

(Luke 12:27-28)

David and Goliath

There was a great big giant named
Goliath who stood 10 feet tall.
He had a mighty sword and was
bigger than them all.
But David was not afraid,
for God said he would be protected.
David used his slingshot
and hit Goliath square in the head.
He defeated the giant,
and the rest of his army fled!
Be brave, because God will protect
you no matter how big or how small
you are.

(1 Samuel 17:32-50)

15

Jesus Dies on the Cross

Jesus was forced to walk up a big hill by an army.
He was then put on a cross between two criminals.
One criminal made fun of Jesus, but the other one said he was sorry.
Jesus died on the cross that day, but He did it to pay for our sins.
He loves us so much that He died so we could be saved!

(Luke 23:26-49)

17

Jesus was put in a tomb. He laid there for three days, and the world was filled with gloom. But then God brought Jesus back to life, and an angel rolled the stone away! He left the tomb and met with His disciples to make sure they would spread the good news. After many weeks, He rose up to Heaven, promising to return someday. But remember His love. He will never let you be alone. So while Jesus is away, He sent the Holy Spirit to always be with you. Whenever you are afraid, remember, you are not on your own.

(Matthew 27:57-28:20)

The Empty Tomb

Lion of Judah

Lions are strong and smart
but gentle to their cubs.
They are great leaders and
great protectors.
Jesus is like a lion, and you
are His cub.
Follow what He says and you
will always be protected.

(Psalm 18:30)

Jesus's Love

The birds fly high in the
big blue sky.
They always have food
and sing songs as they
soar by.
And His love for you is
higher than any bird
could ever fly.
Sing His praise—that's
all you need to do.
When you see a bird up in
the sky, shout at how
high, He must love you!
(Matthew 6:25-34)

23

Gone Fishin'

The disciples went fishing and had no luck. They were about to give up, so Jesus told them to throw their nets on the other side of the boat. The disciples listened, and Jesus was right! Their nets became so full with fish, they barely stayed afloat! When you need help, ask Jesus. He will help you catch whatever you need.
(John 21:1-11)

His Cub

Always remember that
Jesus is a Lion,
and you are His cub.
Jesus breathed life and
made it beautiful, too.
He died on the cross
and paid for your sins.
He did this because
Jesus loves you!

(John 3:16)

Dear Jesus,

Thank you for dying
on the cross for me.
Please forgive me of
my sins and come into
my heart. Be my
Lord and Savior.
I love you.

In your name I pray,
Amen.

Jesus Loves _____HAZEL_____

Age _____4_____

Dear Loved One,

We created this book in hopes that the ones you read it with will come to know the love of Jesus Christ. That they might grow up to share the good news with their friends at school, with their colleagues at work, and one day with a family of their own.

But we also hope that YOU will rediscover your own "childlike faith" and remember the incredible gift of His love and grace. We pray that the message of this book will be with you on your good days and the days you might feel lonely, angry, or confused by the ways of this world. No matter what, just remember: He loves you.

From our hearts to yours,

Noah and Bonnie